# "*Goodbye, Blue-and-Yellow Brick Road*"

## BREXIT- Britain's "Declaration of Independence"

*James Chanel*

# Papermedia

2

### *Also by James Chanel in Papermedia*

### *The Brexit Trilogy*

### *I. Goodbye Blue and Yellow Brick Road. Brexit- Britain's "Declaration of Independence"*

### *II. The Bubble- BREXIT- The Restoration of British Independence & Democracy*

### *III. Brexit in America*

*"The only thing more uncertain than The Future is The Past"*

# 1. *Jokers To The Left, Clowns to The Right...*

My American cousins are always asking me to *"Explain Brexit"*, *"The European Union" and "Cricket"* to them.

I have to disappoint. Most British people don't understand the rules of Cricket. (Even those who play it). Fewer still, understand The EU.

It is only when trying to *explain* The EU, that you realise how absurd, destabilising and manipulative it is. Only with hindsight, once it has collapsed into Civil and Economic War, will the British and others wish they had freed themselves sooner from its grip. Its' economic and political quicksand.

How to untangle "Fact" from er- *Non-Fact.* For we live in an age, in which *"Fact"* and *"Fiction"* have become interchangeable. Indivisible. Their own, Cause and Effect. Where the Media and "Government" are indistinguishable. The Age of *Faction.*

I am an *Independent,* Independent. Was a Government Adviser. But have no "Party". On the basis of Marx (*Groucho* that is not Karl), that I'd never join any Party that would have me as a member.

Perhaps we inherit a lot more in our political DNA than we realize. In 1777, my five times great-grandfather and his brother, rode overnight to Pennsylvania, to witness the adoption of the original *Declaration of Independence.*

Is it some faint echo of "Grandpa Spatz" and his brother, that makes me certain of one thing and one thing only. In this tangled maze, in which not even The EU could now Leave, if it wanted. The EU quagmire is the latest self-destruction of Europe by *Europe*. The West is dying of "Good Intentions".

The Pro-EU Media, Political and Business elites want- *need-* "Independence" from The European Union State to be as *complicated* as they can make it. Obscured. Vague. What kind of *"Brexit"* they ask? BREXIT is a meaningless media-conjured word. Loved by EU Fanatics because they don't have to reveal the true costs- social not just economic of Remaining. A word meaning-less the more it is defined. In the end, there is no *"Hard"* or *"Soft"* Brexit. Only *Independence-* or continued Membership.

*Contrary to the slick Pro-EU propaganda which dominates the corporate media, "British Independence", and that of 28 nations occupied by EU Government, is not "anti-European". Quite the opposite. It has little to do with "Little Englanders" or some blind "nationalism", as has been implanted in the imagination of younger generations.*

*UK Separatists and British Independents are part of a Pan-European Movement for the silenced majorities who want to escape from the corrupt and anti-democratic EU "Soviet" Bloc. Before it stamps itself as a new Federal State from Ireland to The Ukraine, destabilising and Balkanising Europe. Before it becomes Too Big to Fail. When there might be still be a "European Union"- but no Europe.*

"The Four Tests" of a Political and Economic "Independent Nation State". Shared by The US, China, and Australia- and 93% of the big, wide world outside the failing EU Bloc.

Britain isn't "Leaving" Europe- but rejoining the world outside the EU Bubble- the Future.

1. No ***JURISDICTION*** of The EU- its so-called "Parliament" and "Courts". British Laws made by a British Parliament. Government for The British, by the British. Australians or Americans would not stand for their lives being governed and controlled by Romanian or German MEPS they have not elected, sitting in Strasbourg. Why should British voters.

2. ***FREE TRADE*** – Like The US and the rest of the world of independent states. Trading with *Whoever, How* and *When,* The United Kingdom chooses- not via a chaotic Commission of 28 unelected Eurocrats. Paradoxically, economies and their societies work better and are more stable co-operating, but not confined and stunted by Soviet-style Blocs- of which "The EU" is a dying anachronism.

3. ***MIGRATION-*** A competent implementation of an independent, Australian-style VISA Points-based immigration system- matching the economy against migration. Not for some ludicrous, rigid EU ideology of "Free Movement".

4. ***NO FUNDING*** *or Subsidising* of The EU directly or indirectly by stealth. (Propping up the EURO and EU Debt- as the UK currently does via the World Bank and IMF).

*"The Majority- 17,410,742 voters are not "Racist Fascists" simply because they want to live in an independent, self-governing nation again".*

Britain will never be free from The European Union unless its *full Political-* and therefore *Economic-* independence is restored. Until it is once again a fully self-governing, autonomous Nation. The same as The US, China or Australia- even *Burkina Faso-* and 400+ other Independent nation states. Where its laws are made by its Parliament for its Electorate- not someone else's.

Currently, they are grafted on, imported by an unelected Commission and its Euro judges. Remote control rule from Brussels or Luxembourg, just won't work in Bratislava *and* Bracknell. Someone said EU Government it is like pushing on a piece of string.

*"Nothing less than the restoration of sovereignty- as Britain was for a "mere" thousand years- before January 1ˢᵗ 1973. The day when its 45 year experiment with "The EU Project" began".*

In the end, it will not matter whether you are a *"Remainer"* or Leaver. Pro-*this* or Anti-*that.* The EU will collapse, because it is on the wrong side of *History.* Not because of profound democratic issues few understand, and the political elites don't want voters to understand. The EU Project will end due to the *minutiae* of everyday life and running a business. Things that make up those ill-defined, amorphous issues, people can't quite put into words.

Talking of words… The EU will implode, and more quickly than anyone can now imagine, dragging the idea of Europe with it. Why? Because of *detail.* Not the giant frauds going on as we speak- from "Carbon Trading" to Aid programmes. They are easier for The Commission and Council to cover up.

What the public might remember at the voting booth, if by then they still believe in "Voting Booths"- are *details*. That France has 84% of the fish quota in *UK* territorial waters. The EU may collapse because of dead fish- not President Juncker- but the 9.6 million tonnes of fish needlessly dumped because the "EU28" can't even decide, *not* to decide on quotas.

The EU Project will implode because there are 26,911 words of regulations on the production of cabbages- and only about 1,300 in *The US Declaration of Independence*. Because the EU project is *Democratically* unsustainable.

Because even The EU "Thought Police"- The Pro-EU Media- cannot contain the scandal of systemic EU waste, fraud and corruption, forever. The EU's moronic "Leaders" are no longer capable of giving a speech: let alone understanding one like Lincoln's at Gettysburg. And doing it in under 272 words.

Because the *minutiae* of corruption and unaccountability, adds up. A *deficit* of trust. And the £118 billion currently wasted by industry, just proving they *don't* need to comply with EU Directives. And all this *within* the EEA and so-called *frictionless* "Single Market". Pages after page spewed out by Eurocrats... to other Eurocrats. The Eurocracy. Europe's Administration Industry is only fuelling Asia's acceleration. Rule by Technocrats, well-paid to ensure they really *don't* have anything better to do...

If you had to design the worst, most inefficient, way of organising trade and co-ordinating policy among 28 European nations- "The European Union" would be just the disaster you were waiting for.

I have observed the gradual erosion of European Democracy- and quality of life- from afar. In Paris suburbs where police, let alone residents, are now fearful to go out after dusk. As if looking down the wrong end of a telescope. For that is what The European Union does- it *limits* the world. Trade. Innovation. It is parochial "European Isolationism". An inward-looking, Protectionist cartel of nations; buying and selling to one another in a closed and ever-shrinking *"Single Market"*.

*"What the Media Elites and political class do not understand, sitting in the permanent drizzle of Brussels, is that from Singapore and California "The EU" is the Past: not the Future".*

Britain cannot call itself an "independent nation". The sixth largest economy with the global centre that is London, yet it is not "Permitted" by the EU's *Petit-bureaucrats*- The Gnomes of Brussels- to trade freely with The US, China or Australia. Given that 90% of British businesses waste a working day a week on EU paperwork that doesn't apply to them. Capitalism has rusted. Ceased up. How can it function when Eurocrats, not owners, are running businesses.

Every British family is forced to pay the net EU subsidy- to build new motorways in Slovakia and pay Spanish farmers *not* to grow anything. Even after so-called "rebates"- of its own taxpayers' money- the UK Government wastes an average £10 billion on its annual transfusion. Just to keep the EU corpse and its Zombie currency, The Euro, on life support. While voters are told the UK doesn't have "enough" for its own crumbling social, educational and transport, infrastructure. (Also wasting £13.6 billion annually on Foreign Aid to prop up corrupt African and Asian regimes).*"Austerity"* becomes unjustifiable given such flagrant Government waste.

Though the Elites do not realise it yet, the UK and the voiceless millions trapped within the EU, are now beyond Democratic "breaking point". Ministers should try standing for two hours on a dangerously overcrowded commuter train- and pay £6000 annually for the privilege. You can cut the anger in the air with a knife on the platform waiting for the 7.31 which will not arrive. They do not queue outside hospitals where the old are left to defecate in their beds.

EU "membership" costs every family approximately £3100 a year. Families who can't afford to heat their houses or go on holiday- to Europe. Contrary to the media myth, Britain doesn't get anything "back" from The EU. It is with British taxpayers *own* money that they are bribed into Remaining. Funds which can't be spent as, when and how, *their* own MPs and elected representatives choose. On EU "Mickey Mouse" projects. All filtered through layers of tangled EU administration, duplicated agencies and corruption.

### *Welcome to the EUSSR…*

The broken promises of Reform. A "EU State Constitution" pretending to be only "Treaties", the *"mere"* public doesn't need to worry it itself about. Just let the Eurocrats decide for you. Understand for you. Vote for You. The same trick EU Fanatics are using now to limit the restoration of British Independence. Until there is only one option- the same EU membership rebranded for younger generations. Those who have not watched the systematic erasure of Britain since 1973.

It began before I suppose, in school, when in 1973 our maps of *"Great Britain"* were surreptitiously replaced by photocopies of

"European Community" maps. We are not dotty "Nostalgics" for *"The Great"*, as the Pro-EU lobby think they can dismiss us. Or *ignore* us into submission. It is the EU that wants to divide "The United Kingdom", so like all Empire builders, it may conquer. It is the EU declaration of Civil War. And our "Unilateral Declaration of Independence"- from the EU State.

The subtle brainwashing had begun. But I used to cross out the *"EC"*. And always will. How would an American citizen feel- or an Australian or Chinese- if when they renewed their passport to suddenly find *"EUROPEAN UNION"* stamped in gold letters above and over your country. Of another country, you were never asked or wanted to become a "Citizen" of. We became "State-less" overnight. Colonised by stealth. By an unelected, corrupt bureaucracy. Directive by Directive. By allowing our so called "Leaders"- the ones we never voted for- to create, perhaps deliberately create, a political vacuum to be filled by *"Ever Closer Union"*.


*"The EU will implode. Not If but When. If only because 500 million EU passport holders, cannot live and settle in each others countries. Not everyone can live in a few, leafy South-West London suburbs- on a direct tube line"*.

The Pro-EU Media invented the perfect euphemism- *"Brexit"*- to describe the indescribable. It's like asking "How long is a piece of string?". A distraction. Anything- rather than use the dirty "I" word *"Independence"*. They will talk and talk about Everything and Anything rather than the issue of restoring full "National Independence". There is no *"Hard"* or *"Soft"* Brexit- because there is no "Brexit". Only political and economic National Independence *or* EU membership. There is no sliding scale of *Sovereignty*, despite what the Euromaniacs want to believe. Like "Flat-earthers" trying to convince others by convincing themselves. The EU is itself- a conspiracy without a Theory.

The EU can only fail because it defies both Social and Economic reality. The average hourly wage in Romania and Bulgaria is about £2. (Now Britain's largest Immigrant groups- up from 7,301 in 2001 to 413,000 in 2017). If you can get a job. The UK Minimum Wage equates to being paid about £20 an hour. That is why *Easy-jet* flights *from* Bucharest are full. But oddly only a few thousand British are choosing to use their Right to "Free Movement", and live in now a deserted village in The Carpathians. Grasp that, and you see The Future of EU- it hasn't one.

Few of the indigenous unemployed, weaned off benefits, wouldn't work all hours cleaning toilets, making prawn sandwiches and vacuuming office carpets. All three jobs, if like migrants, they were paid the equivalent of £20 per hour in their own country.

The indigenous British cannot always "afford" to work 60 hours a week, for an extra £10 more than they would get on benefits. Their own Government policy has deliberately hooked them on welfare. (And disproportionality high National Insurance and tax rates). Pro-EU business is more than happy to cream off the profit in between, with an endless supply of Eastern European and migrant labour. Creating its very own caste of "Untouchables"- to do Europe's dirty work.

The absurdity of an "elected Government" being unable, *and or* unwilling, to control immigration while within in The EU. Since the 1950's, successive Cabinets have played pass-the-parcel with migration. Until the public no longer trust the statistics- nor the Government that rigs them. They have no faith left in the ability of *any* Home Office, to actually administer a competent immigration system. As they manage to do in Australia or Canada being fully independent nation states. Not locked into two competing, contradictory, legal systems and *Governments* within The European Parliament, Council and its farcical "Court of Justice".




*"Civil Wars occur when both sides, as in Brexit, believe they are being 'Patriotic".*

The problem the British now face, as ever, isn't The Problem. It's being 50 years too late. But then what can you except from a cabinet of failed lawyers, turned failed PR men, like Blair and Cameron. The disaster of PM Brown, who wouldn't have made an average Vice-Chancellor of a provincial Scottish University- in a bad year. *"Call-me-Dave"*, who I remember from Conservative Central Office; lolling on a swivel chair, feet up on the table eating a sandwich, and being *charming*. His "Direct line", on a faded *Post-it* note, is still stuck to a page of an old diary. People even then tipped "Dave"- and another three Old Etonians- as future Prime Ministers-in-waiting. See The Problem? He was "Eye-candy"- I remember one blonde Party Bimbo enthusing. Another, now famous blond male Bimbo, turned Foreign Secretary, interviewed me for a Research job…

The British have only had the last two centuries to reform their failed socio-political system, that suits so few, so well. The mediocrity, the drift of post-war politics, is proof of what happens if you do not include the A-political. The *independents*. If you write-off 90% of your population before they even start school. They say you never forget a good teacher. Well, you never forgive a bad school. Or a country that screws you up into the bin.

The British have dross- worse *incompetent* dross- in their Government and much of public life, because decades before, they did not open up the oyster-like self-selecting elites of Left and Right. The cliques-within-cliques of The Media. But I suspect, people don't want to know what they put into The Party sausage machine.

Human nature. Grim economic realities will always- if you excuse the pun- *Trump* the Theory of The EU. Its rigid, nonsensical "Pillars". Maastricht *Principles*. Which, like the *Dublin Migration Accords*- migrants should register in the first country of arrival- the German Government disregards. When it suits a Chancellor's Poll ratings. Until an election approaches.

Inviting 2 million migrants to reach "German soil" to become German, "EU Citizens", and therefore potential British citizens. Making jackpot Euro millionaires of Traffickers in their new, growth industry. The mass media hysteria. The self-destructive, collective insanity. All this is at the root of why their German "EU Project" can only fail.

Supermarkets, business and manufacturing should be filled with a wide range of world-sourced goods- not economically asphyxiated by the protectionist EU cartel. Limiting world trade, innovation, consumer choice and price. And would be, but for punitive anti-competitive EU tariffs and hurdles, to emerging economies in Africa an India as well as The US and Australasia. The UK as one of the world leading G7 economies is suffocated by not being "permitted" to trade freely and directly with China or The US. It has to go via the maze of the "EU28" for *approval*.

Indeed "Deals" with The EU are the kiss of death. A straitjacket. It's why China and The US don't have one. Britain, as huge net importer of £200 million goods from the EU, reveals that France, Germany and Spain et al- have good reason to maintain the *status quo*. With the collusion of "HM Government" they will con the British public again, into believing they have "left" The EU, and are once more, an independent nation.

*"The more the EU fails- the more its fanatical supporters and acolytes believe in it. It is "The Blue-and-Yellow Brick Road" at the end of which is Jean Claude Juncker as The Wizard of Oz".*

Those outside the "EU Bubble" can see more clearly, the *"Titanic EU"* disaster waiting to happen. The iceberg of the "Single Currency" looms dark on the horizon. One Federal, German-dominated ECB Central Bank, trying the herd the bag of cats of 28 members, with as as many disparate economic and political structures. Impossible. The EU Fantasy cannot be sustained. The Four "Freedoms" have become Europe's prison. Ironically, Europe would be more stable today had the EU never existed. Evidenced by Austria coming close to conflict with Slovenia in 2016. Europe's epitaph will surely be *"Ever Closer Union"*.

It is the clearest example of the idealogical lunacy of The EU: trying to override cultural and economic realities of ordinary people trying to make a living and their children into schools. Politicians are reluctant to believe that *"Government"* is part of The Problem- not The Solution. With their algorithms and social media, they have fooled themselves into believing their own Fake News. So sophisticated, that they forget that *reality* not Democracy, will always out last them. As those who blindly support "EU Appeasement" of the Federal Fascism of The EU State, have learnt nothing from the 1930's.


*The EU can only shatter, self-destruct, because it is on the wrong side of History. Its Council, like King Canute, trying to hold back an Asian world economic tide. The Asian technological tsunami.*

See how the EU oligarchs get its captive member states, like Greece, Hungary and Ireland, hooked on "EU grants", then "Subsidies", and finally ECB debt. Then they bully by threatening Sanctions, withdrawal of voting rights. Invading supposedly independent nations with their embryonic EU Army "Border Force". So when Ireland or Hungary wants to control its own economic or border policy, its destiny has already been lost ten years before, to The Eurocracy.

*We already know from History, what History will remember about the aborted, 50 year "EU Experiment". That EU "Integration" only divided. Its obsession with Solidarity, destroyed it. And striving for Peace created Civil War.*

The UK is best disentangled from the spaghetti of The EU. Its addictive subsidies, wasteful structures and corrupt programmes. As the EU *Super-nova* expands too far, then collapses, into a Black Hole of recrimination, Social *dis-integration,* and miniaturised Wars, in Slovenia and along the Turkish border.

*"Europe is now only ever one election away from Civil War".*

For now, the EU debate is still at the level of "shopping"- the British addiction-come-leisure activity. The main fear seems to be, as I overheard in one supermarket, will they be able to buy "Those nice Italian *Amaretti* biscuits" after Brexit?"... But what can one expect from a semi-educated, sports obsessed nation whose "History" begins and ends at 1966.

But perhaps that *is* what matters. Not "Democracy". But the minutiae that composes a life. A life they have forgotten how to live within a free Nation state. And businesses survive without the protectionist greenhouse of Euro subsidies. The real world, real productivity, outside the Nanny-knows-Best "EU Superstate". Our spineless bureaucrats should wait until the smell of overripe French cheese starts to waft across the Channel- its biggest market. Then talk about "Deals" or No Deals.

The Truth that dare not speak its name is that, in practice, the UK will not be able to trade freely with the outside world; or control its borders and migration in any kind of "Deal" or *"Arrangement"* with the EU. Marketed to a public who will just want to get on earning a living, to go on subsidising a permanently bankrupt EU.

*Bizarrely, Britain has more in common with the US and New Zealand, than it does with The EU just 21 miles across the- English-Channel.*

Now that the EU mask has slipped, it has revealed itself as the Anti-democratic monolith that it is. The genii of the *Independence Movement* is out of its tightly screwed bottle. However much its diktats are sugared as being "Environmental". Bitter economic medicine for your own good.

The silenced *vox populi* might decide it has no choice but bypass "Parliamentary Chambers" and *"Debate"* silenced by the EU regime. And begin waving- or burning- its blue-and-yellow flags. The wildfire of Civil War. The European Chaos has already begun. The failure of Europe not by Revolution. But by sheer *naivety*.

*That is why silenced millions want to Leave The EU straitjacket. Not only for what The EU is now. But before it accelerates, ever more desperate to survive, into a Federal "United States". The EU State that can only exist by erasing Nation states and their identities.*

## 2. The EU- Europe's Frankenstein

*"A Nation cannot be a little bit "Independent". Any more than you can be "somewhat Pregnant". "Brexit" can only mean- British laws made in a Free British Parliament by British MPs. Anything less is de facto Membership".*

If Britain does not leave now- it never will. It will in effect cease to exist as a fully self-governing, Independent nation. The country formerly known as "The United Kingdom", will slide inexorably into being one of 28 "Provinces". "Economic Colonies", like Greece, of the emerging EU State. The poorest and the unemployed in the East, used as a vast, borderless "labour camp" for the EU core nations- in practice- Germany. To build all those *Volkswagen* city-cars The Workers will want loans to buy- with someone else's, hard-earned cash...

The EU Project is tale of Unintended Consequences. In which *"Integration"* has only resulted in division. *"Diversity"* has ended in suspicion and enmity, as governments scramble to undo, what due to apathy, they haven't done. Unrolling razor wire across borders and patrolling rivers between two *ideas* of Europe.

*"Independence"* means national Representatives directly making a nation's own laws, for its population- not someone else's. *True "Independence"*- not the faux-Independence Eurocrats talk of, is not divisible. Contrary to what they will assure you- Democratic

"Sovereignty" cannot be *shared*. You can't be a "little bit pregnant". Democracy is diluted by the EU's parallel government.

A semi-educated public, pummelled by constant stream of Pro-EU "reporting", do not understand- have time to understand the *reality* of EU membership. Busy working as they are to pay ever-rising stealth Taxes to fund it. Few realise that their own "Parliament" is not the same as the "EU Parliament". That unelected Judges in the European Courts- essentially derived from the "French Revolutionary" system- *make* Laws. Or can ignore them.

That only 28 unelected EU Commissioners are permitted to introduce laws into the EU Parliament for over 500 million to live under. The toothless EU Parliament of "political eunuchs" is a clever charade. Window-dressing for Eurocratic dictatorship. Whereas in Westminster- for all its *many* faults- any MP can introduce legislation. Often prompted by constituents. Barely 2% of voters even know who *their* MEP or Commissioner is. Or the difference between *"The European Council"* and "EU Council of Ministers". Me neither.

The EU is inherently anti-Democratic. MEP's of The EU "Eurocracy" are "elected" with less than 10% of the vote. With turnouts frequently below 20%. Polling Stations without any voters at all. You are either an Independent Nation- as China or Australia is. Or a Member Colony of The EU. Not both. As any Greek will tell you. Who knows now, to beware Germans bearing gifts…

*"Wealth never "Trickles Down". It always waterfalls- upwards".*

Euro Extremists like to cite the example of "The United States", as the "model" for how *The United States of Europe* will one day be. When they reach the end of *The Blue-and-Yellow Brick Road…*

Then they miss out 200 years of History. American Federalism is no perfection. The Mason-Dixon Line is alive and *kickin*. It cannot be superimposed on Europe. Even Washington's "Federalism" looks very different in those other "Americas". In the silent Ghost Towns of the coal and Rust Belts of Pennsylvania. In *Sweet Home Alabama.* In a Neo-Hispanic New Mexico.

In the Southern, former  "Confederate" States there remains, an echo. An unhealed resentment of its annexation by the "Union North". Where the procession of grey ghosts of the Civil War, still walk South in search of America. As Europe become "Balkanised" in its way, will the ghosts of Europe's coming Civil War be walking for as long into the future? Which way will they go- North or South?

For it is not what the The EU is *now*- but will be- that voters must vote for now. If they are "allowed" that much "Democracy". As The European Union's Bureaucratic, Little Empire stretches, from the windswept coast of the West of Ireland, where you might walk all day and see no sign of what Continent you are on, America or Europe. To the icy border of the Ukraine; where border guards still cock their Kalashnikov as soon as look at you... The question is, which way will they point- East or West?

# 3. The EU's "Four Pillars" of Insanity

As soon as The Berlin Wall came down, I travelled West to East. It made me see The EU obliquely. Differently from University contemporaries cosseted on *Erasmus* programmes and making a name for themselves as lawyers in Strasbourg once a month. Commuting on the Brussels "Red Eye", expenses paid, is a very different *"European Union"*, from Poznan and the former Eastern Germany. As in the name of *Integration,* they supplanted one Communism for another- EU Communism.

I boarded the sleeper train at the *Gare D'est,* nominally in search of a story about "Red Mercury". (Me neither- used in nuclear trigger devices). Several papers had been tipped-off. But news-wire agencies- as they were known- and *Reuters* didn't normally lower itself, chasing second-hand rumours of rumours.

So they sent "Stringers" and nobodies in search of something. Even lowly Stringers like me, the London loose end of a Parisian newspaper. Picking up gossip in a bar in Prague. In university refectories and halls of residence, where students had just completed their National Service. Rumour which, if it turned out to be little more than a hoax, the trusted legitimate sources could deny having got it wrong. And if it turned out true- could take the credit for the Scoop. Just about Everything was being smuggled via Kiev. Whispers of the Red Mercury pointed to a former Soviet naval base, where officers hadn't been paid in two years and some still lived on their rusty submarines. But that really is *another* story. But the trip did make me see the EU Illusion for what it was. A mirage of Democracy.

As with all stories- it gave birth to another. The story within. The one you hadn't meant to write. It made me think about The Russian *matryoska* doll. One inside another. And how "The European Union" revealed itself. Expanded. Metamorphosed into a Federal *"United States of Europe"*.

The EU Project may look haphazard. Don't be fooled. It is all Game Theory. Win-Win. Lose-Lose. An accidental Federal State will be created by default. Because in the coming war with Russia, it will seem to a desperate public like the lessor of two evils. Especially by excluding America who won't be rescuing The Europeans again from their own stupidity.

The EU imposes its Ideology first through "Co-operation". Then, emboldened by its own arrogant self-belief, in ever more obvious Economic warfare. As the EU crumbles, its Ruling Elites will only accelerate towards the political suicide note of *"Ever Closer Union"*. How long before its "President" and "EU Foreign Minister" decide to mobilize their Euro Army along the Swedish or Baltic borders. Always a good distraction when Elections, if not Russian tanks, loom on the horizon.

Silent millions are trapped inside the EU Economic Prison. Politicians and voters unable to take the short-tern economic hit to escape. Even if, like the UK they will save £180bn according to the ERG over 15 years. Billions wasted on net EU contributions, self-defeating tariffs, in exports and industries restricted by EU membership.

Millions of voters do not know they are Prisoners of the EU. The politically illiterate, paying their ever rising taxes to keep obese, corrupt "Euro Project" fed. For the Union cannot be *"Reformed"*. Or even dismantled. Not without Civil War. That is the EU Oligarchs "Trump" card- always to present a worse alternative. The EU as the lessor of two evils. A poor reason for remaining inside The EU Bubble.

*"Just because a politician takes his jacket off, doesn't mean he is A Man of The People"*

The quicksand of EU Regulation is often dressed up as *"Environmental"*. Or as nebulous benefits to the "little European" consumer, versus the Big Bad American corporate. Always camouflaged, as something no one can argue with without being typecast as "Adolf Eichmann". Like "saving refugees", who once out of an inflatable dinghy, become "Economic Migrants" as soon as they are given a flat outside Gothenburg and free dental care.

The example of *Apple* in Ireland, reveals the truth behind the EU's "Alt-Communism". Attracted by the Republic's low Corporate Tax rates, Apple set up base. So far so good. Eventually, even the EU oligarchs began smelling rather a lot of juicy Tax, that wasn't being filtered via them. They decided to get their attack dogs in their "Court of Justice". (All Commission appointed "Judges") To rule that *Apple* – for the crime of being both Successful *and* American- "owed" Ireland 13 billion Euros. Jealous of Ireland's lower competitive Tax rates, Germany among others, dictated that rates be *raised t*o "harmonize" with their own. *"Harmonize Europe"*- where have we heard that one before?

The result- *"The EU 1- Capitalist Free Market 0"*. Nil points. It was The EU's own-goal.

Ireland's supposedly "Sovereign" elected government had to refuse the 13 billion. Or accept Germany's tax rates. As ever, The EU's

*Hobson's choice,* beggar thy neighbour, tactic. Such is the madness for which 16 million voted *Remain.* Just blame The Madness on *Post-traumatic Distress Disorder-* or a Gluten-free diet, like everything else. *Enjoy.*

Similarly, as any Boeing executive will tell you, the grossly inefficient EU Airbus Project, in which wing parts are needlessly transferred back and forth across The Channel four times, for no technical production reason, other than to satisfy an ideal of EU *"Solidarity".* Airbus would not survive in the Outside world, without its bottomless EU Taxpayer subsidies. *Welcome to the EUSSR...*


*"If "None of The Above" were added to ballot slips- it would currently be occupying "No.10"- not the succession of squatter Governments "elected" with only 23% of the vote".*

Indeed, the European Project was founded to undermine American imports and industry. This inward-looking, spitefulness has only made European industry less innovative and responsive to global markets. It is why The British and their City financial markets, never belonged inside the EU Cartel. But also why France and Germany primarily, wanted to entrap and squeeze London's Square Mile dry. It is curious how the policy of envy lies within wider, hidden national agendas. Perhaps even a hint of latent anti-Semitism, underscoring anti-American sentiment in EU institutions. As I have heard at dinner parties of French intelligentsia, in the leafy *arrondissements* of the Sorbonne.

"Generation Euro" have been told- all "Nationalism Bad". "European Integration Good". That "The European Union" *is Europe.* Simplistic answers are how Dictatorships *dictate-* Liberal Dictatorships included.

The Comfortable. The well-meaning Naive. The Spoilt Luvvies. They can see no harm in sharing, donating *Sovereignty*. Other people's Sovereignty. That's the problem with defending the idea of the "Nation State". The reason for it, its benefits, are only noticed once they are lost. Systemically erased. As the increasingly authoritarian Union has attempted across Europe since 1957.

# 4. *The EU Oligarchs*

We trundled towards "The East" in 1990, and into The Past. It was as if the The Europe of "1945", and Soviet Ideology remained frozen, in the snow-covered wooden sheds of the Collectivist farms and silent factories; making things no one had wanted, or could buy. The arm of Stalin's statue on the thin, grey horizon, pointing skywards- as if to an Idea in concrete.

Which side was *which?* I wondered. So used as we are, to "Goodies" and "Baddies". Beginnings and Endings. But outside the train window, and inside everything was in shades of grey.

Which the most danger in the end? To that partial, ever flexing *instability*. The compromise we call *"Democracy"*. Between the Have-too-much- and *Have-nots*. Those who *Know*. And those who think they know better. The EU's moribund leadership always reminds me of "Experts". There are only two kinds- those who don't know The Answers. And, much more dangerous, those who don't *know* they don't know.


*"Chinese, Americans, Australians wouldn't tolerate their laws, regulations and migration policy, being dictated by a tiny elite; a few hundred unelected Technocrats far away in Berlin, Brussels or Strasbourg. Yet this is what "The Unelected Commission" demands-*

*obedience from the silenced millions, who do not want- were never asked- if they wanted to be "Citizens" of a European Union".*

The Pro-EU Elites have superimposed their "Euro Group-think". Federalism has been subtly, deviously repackaged. Rebranded. By soft, media power. Through "Education" and "Aid" programmes. No one could possibly disagree with "The Good" that EU programmes were doing, could they? As 8 in 10 so-called "Refugees" arriving in Germany were found by the UNHCR to be economic migrants. Barely 1% will ever be repatriated. For unless bribed with Dollars, which country is going be as stupid and gullible as *Mutti* Merkel's Germany? Her naivety will now be transposed on the poorest of British Taxpayers, as waves of the Neo-Europeans head West...

Building on its sclerotic foundations another Communist Bloc in the middle of Western Europe. Some would even say, the latest incarnation of Germany's economic, then political, "Fourth Reich". European integration into an "EU State" is as dangerously arrogant as any "Empire"- Soviet or Islamic or Liberal Consumerist.

I am no apologist for "Russia Plc". Or of the current quagmire of "Liberal Extremism" and Apathy in which the West is determined to drown itself. The "Hyper-tolerance" to Everything and Anything that has only generated a resurgent Globalised, Right Wing. The "Alt-Ego" opposite of The EU. A smokescreen the EU can, as ever, blame rather than deal with its own systemic corruption and incompetence.

For there is nothing worse than a Liberal scorned. Those, so proud of being "reasonable-minded". "Open". Discovering at long last, that they can allow themselves to *Hate* something. Simply by eagerly slapping a *"Populist"* label on a shaven head.

The straitjacket of its domed Single Currency- the worthless Euro. A counterproductive Migration, *Non*-Policy. Trying to foment hostility, even conflict, with the Russian Federation. Antagonising its people, US allies, and other nations. Rather than being an example to it. Starting by, rooting out endemic corruption and waste in its own EU agencies and structures. A set of public accounts, properly audited not by its own *"Court of Auditors"*, might be a start. Before Brussels dictates to others how *not* to be a "Banana Republic"- as The EU is.

## *The Seven Myths of the European Union*

The bankrolled *Remain* campaign had an acquiescent media. HM Treasury preprepared biassed reports for it, courtesy of the taxpayer. And still failed to win the argument. Because they they lost it when the Euro was still-born in 1992. Ideas born on spreadsheets don't make good reality.

EU Extremists can now blame pre-existing NHS and business staffing shortages- rainy summers, losing the World Cup- and *anything* they can think of on "Brexit". It's the perfect excuse. The distraction of all distractions.

The same merry-go-round of systemic social and economic problems- can now be conveniently blamed ever after on *"Brexit"*. A word "Tweedledee and Tweedledee Dummer" might have invented. A word which no one can agree what it means- except that it means *everything* to *everyone*.

"Experts" fill every channel. Sound-bites are on loops. Politicians are people who are good at pretending they know, when they haven't a clue. Worse still are those experts who don't *know*, they don't know.

Even they can't define what *"Brexit"* is- or isn't. Ask two Economist and get three equally incorrect answers. Because what the powers that be don't want to admit- yet- is that Brexit has only one meaning. It can in the end, at the 59<sup>th</sup> minute of the eleventh hour of "negotiations" *only* mean full political *and* economic *Independence*.

But the Elites, "The EU Diktats", want what the British have done since the 1950's, when the EU Project began to take root- to *blur*. *Avoid*. Compromise. The usual "English Fudge"- that has put off the problem of "Europe" for five decades. When Great Britain swapped ambivalence for its fading Imperial role for a seat at the Euro "High Table". No longer can, "Cans be kicked down roads"... So they talk of Anything but the "I word". Restoring *Independence*. To be a free country once again.

*"BREXIT" means the UK becoming "Australia", The US and like 400 other nation states- an Independent country again. Its incompetent politicians and leaders know they aren't up the job of governing. They've had 45 years of avoidance- hiding behind the EU edifice".*

Because The British mentality, and disease, is always *short-termism*. Politicians have a sort of forward-amnesia- they forget in advance. Never investing in education, training, for three decades time- only the next three months until The Election. Their Sacred Cow- Welfare and the British *Nationalised* Health service cannot be sustained. The latter because it was designed in a Britain in 1948 which no longer exists. And *ssh* don't tell them- but it is an unsustainable way of delivering healthcare in 2018. Because unfortunately- it's not about The Money.


*As they say- that's trouble with "Happiness"- it can't buy you Money.*

That, and the UK "Welfare-Migration" industry will end up bankrupting the UK state- and the inevitable, long overdue, run on Sterling. Britain simply can't afford to be *Britain*. As migrant families expand, drawing in more migration, requiring more services, the social and economic stitching of the islands with a population topping 66 million will split. The OECD calculated that the UK optimum sustainable population was 50 million. Unreported by the EU's Channel- *The BBC*.

The truth is that successive administrations have avoided investing in apprenticeships and *employable* skills for their indigenous population- while encouraging breastfeeding programmes in Bulgaria and paying for Girl Bands in Kenya. Easier to import someone else's brightest and best than make your own. English teenagers and under-30's are The Great Ignored. White Working Class Boys- the least likely to go on to college. Yet they don't have BBC Producers fawning over them. Trying to *understand* them, in a syrupy caramel of Middle Class, Oxbridge guilt and *empathy*. Or have their own dedicated Channel. That would be *Racist*. They don't make Good TV. They're not *User-friendly*. Except to bait the Right Wing into saying something stupid, the media can then edit into a self-condemning sound-bite.

"Generation Euro" is caught between being "European" and unable to be white *and* British. They know Taylor Swift's lyrics backwards– but can't string a sentence together. Not *like* without five *likes*. Perhaps they lack the confidence of *Identity*- American and Australian children possess.

For the Westerners everything is coloured a muddy shade, a moral grey of relativism. Belief in *Everything* and *Anything*- and therefore Nothing. Discarding the dirty words of *Tradition*. And the media self-definition of *"Nationalism"*. Trying to rub out the "stains" of the past- has only ingrained them.

It is as if The British have forgotten- *Who* they are. *What* they are for. Did they ever? Searching and adopting a hybrid *European-ness*- only to find that too is illusory. Holding placards proclaiming they are *"European"* not British- is in fact a sign of the failure of The European project.

The British seem haunted by their own Past. One they can't even learn at school. Unless denigrated, diluted by some Liberal algorithm. The PC filtering of inconvenient truths. Historians shouldn't get too *Historical* about it. Even if amateur TV Historian Dan Snow, lies to his daughters that "women flew in combat in the Battle of Britain". His excuse, as crass as it is self-defeating- that it "empowers" them.

History is being rewritten not by the "Victors"- but by those *oh-so* reasonable, level-headed Liberals. Luvvies thinking they are only Doing Good- by lying. Little White Lies. At first. How odd future generations will think we are. That no one dare complain in the media that a black actor portrayed US Founding Father Alexander Hamilton. Who, contrary to media hype was not "Black". Not even "7/8ths" true. If a white actor were to play Dr. King there would be outrage. Proof that whatever your view, *Ideology* is being taught- not History.

*As an outsider looking in, The Invisible English are the only sub-group- a "minority" now in many towns- that is not indulged and pampered. An endangered species no one wants to conserve.*

On the other side of the Euro coin, countries like Romania and Poland have in effect exported their unemployment. And all the social welfare costs- to Britain. Do you think Romania or Bulgaria's Presidents would still be in power with 25% unemployment were it not for Open Migration.

This also keeps the unemployment rate in the UK higher and wages lower. No incentive to "up skill" your workforce when you can simply put on more Easy-jet t flights from Skopje. The problem for the British is *under*-employment. The hidden costs of keeping people out of work, so that a few can *overwork*. They do not use a fraction of their national talent: but squander it and their future. They can't resist the pull of cheap labour- while cotton-wooled inside the EU28.

In The EU, in practice, HM Government isn't *Her Majesty's*. The UK can't have an independent Migration, Trade or Economic policy. In reality, for the last decade Interest rates have been set in Frankfurt- not by the Bank of England. Especially with less than useless, vehement EU puppet in Governor Carney. Anyone with a PhD in Economics should be automatically debarred from running a Central Bank.

In Britain, it is the second and third generations migrants who have the most to lose remaining in the coming EU State. Pakistani and Chinese families who object most to Open Migration. They are paying the price for politicians idealism and Luvvies' sound-bites. Easy to get cheap applause on a BBC *Question Time* panel. To play The Mob- rather than take razor-sharp decisions to exit the EU. Before it becomes the behemoth of the coming United States of Europe. Decisions that will, in the short term, hurt equally- Remain or Leaver.

The myth that a *"Meaningful Vote"* isn't about preventing the UK democratic majority vote to Leave the EU. Though they don't want to admit it- "Leave" can only mean full UK Independence. Or turn the "Palace of Westminster" into a Five star hotel. Or perhaps a *Museum to Democracy*. The usual British "Compromise" will only makes things worse. For that is what its membership of the Euro Project since 1973 has been. An uneasy *compromise*.

This fear of national Independence, will precipitate a long overdue split in all parties. The "Political Party" simply isn't fit-for-purpose in the Internet Age of Anti-Social Media. The Party's over. Even the "best" politicians are at best, mediocre.

A vote of *"No Confidence"* will fell several Prime Ministers. A succession of leadership challenges and Elections follows. A "Meaningful Vote" means a Second Referendum. Why not a third. Why not re-run the General Election, if the margin is only 4%, and The Media Mob decide it doesn't like the result. The result it hadn't been able to rig by its "impartial" reporting.

The trouble is, as a recent survey revealed, 98% of Media voted "Remain" or define themselves as "Pro-EU". However "Professional" they think they are- in reality their address books tend to be full of mobile numbers of the same like-minded pundits, they met at dinner parties in Hampstead the week before. An echo-chamber of Luvvies talking to Luvvies. It's why the Referendum shocked them so. As the future will even more. As our job-less, home-less grandchildren will likely be more socially "conservative" than their grandparents. As they see how the EU and blinkered social liberalism of their parents has failed them. Still believing in The EU Dream. Even as the edges of Europe crumble, and their social framework, frays and splinters.

The heavy hand of The EU State is already crushing any shoots of dissent. Buying off Hungary's opposition parties and electorates with promises of investment, jobs, Visa-free travel and a nice new flat in Düsseldorf...

Deciding Poland's judiciary for it. Vetoing Judges appointed by a nominally "sovereign" government. So that Pro-EU judges will later rubber-stamp Brussels' Migrant Quotas. Then "Resettlement" labour camps dotted across Eastern Europe. The Berlin Plan to import a ready made labour-force for German industry. VW is already building factories in Turkey- as Germany overspills the EU borders East and West. And one wonders, how long before an EU

NATO Army deployed as a temporary "emergency" measure, to "protect" Ukraine. From what exactly? The future.

In the end- the British will have to face the many "elephants" they have been avoiding for so long. Crammed onto their tiny isle. Creating generations of the unemployable- "Generation *Selfie-ish*". A highly-educated, self-aware- but mostly unemployable elite of narcissists.

In a panic they will as The Netherlands had to, introduce a Privatised healthcare insurance system. What will their flaccid politicians do when they can no longer blame those funny Little Gnomes in Brussels and Luxembourg, letting their *manekin pis* all over them. They will actually have to Do something.

Parliament could not decide- *The Europe Problem.* So it off-loaded responsibility for the inevitable cock-up it would have made anyway- onto the Good Old British Public. Then call them stupid sheep for deciding "Wrong", after 45 years of In-Out debate about "Europe".

Its time for The Emperors New Clothes. To see the naked EU. That Britain would have been better off since 1973 outside the EU Cartel. Europe would be safer, better administered, and more competitive. Sadly, "The People" have always preferred sugar-coated Lies today, than the bitter Truth tomorrow.

# 5. Vox Populist

So far, The EU has expanded and survived, only through the gritted teeth of Toleration of millions who never wanted, were never asked, if they wanted to be EU Citizens.

*"The Declaration of British Independence"* sets out clearly "What Brexit" means. The only sustainable "Brexit" is the restoration of pre-1973 UK Independence- to the same status as the US, China, Australia and 300 other Free States.

***1. "Independence" means there must be no subsidies- direct or indirectly- of The EU or EURO debts.***

***2. No imposition of EU laws, Court jurisdiction or Regulation- overtly or by stealth.***

***3. A Free British Parliament. The same as any independent Nation State- that decides with Whom and How- it will trade.***

***4. The adoption- and competent management- of an "Australian Points-based Visa" system to match Migration to the Economy. Ending the imposition of EU ideology such as "Free Movement", rooted in its Socialistic foundation and the world of the 1950's.***

In the UK Referendum, the culmination of 50 years of see-saw debate, HM Government wasted £8 million of taxpayers' own money, producing a Pro-EU Propaganda leaflet. Clearly listing all the *certain* "Dangers" of Leaving, and only the "Virtues" of being Good EU Citizens, doing what you are told- and *Vote Remain.* Ending with the line, that took down a Prime Minister- *"The Government will implement your decision".*

The Prime Minister and Chancellor, saturated every channel for months. Bemused, then panicking that they couldn't repeat the same "Three-Card EU Con trick" again. Repeating the EU Mantra, like parrots in well-tailored suits. Then The Elites and Big Business resorted to scaremongering, bullying. Ironically if the EU was "working", if it were Democratic, it wouldn't require a Referendum. Though some waited 40 years for the "Privilege", it was a sign of failure of the whole bizarre and pointless EU Project.

And still a majority, voted against the tide. The mass Pro-EU propaganda. And still the Elites will not listen. Not until tyres are burnt on the streets and police cars overturned. Even with a 2-4% in-built bias in favour of the "Vote Remain" status Quo. It is easy to Vote "Yes". To be *liked* on Facebook. To glow in the knowledge of what a tolerant, "Open" minded member of the human race you are. Meanwhile, in real life… When you need a job. *Any* job. When your mother with cancer, can't get a GP appointment until the week after next week- "at the earliest".

As the Euromaniacs "Remain" in Denial- the Real world and Asia moves on. While the British faff about a "Third Runway" for Heathrow- by 2015 China will have built *136* new airports. The British cannot live forever on the fat of their Imperial and Industrial Revolution past.

*Paradoxically, the over-hyped "benefits" of being part of an EU Bloc, whose power is miraculously greater than the sum of its parts, will prove just another lie of the European illusion.*

While The Commission's unelected "representatives" debate, how much qualifies as *"Qualified Majority Voting"*. Juncker and his EU Mafia cronies, are like Mediaeval Popes arguing over *"How many Angels can dance on the end of pin"*...

The 85% Pro-EU Parliament has never been "Representative" of the real electorate. Only 4 in 10 elect their Government in any case. *Parliament* itself voted for a Referendum, because Parliament admitted it was not competent to "Decide"- *In* or *Out.* So when Government thought the economy was strong enough to win safely, it shifted the responsibility of making a Decision- to the public in a Referendum. That way, whichever way they voted- the voters would get the blame.

The public spoke, only to be insulted by being told- *"They didn't know what they were voting for"*. After 45 years of broken promises, creeping Federalism, Euro financial crisis after crisis- they *knew*.

As they *know* when their MP tells them "There's no Money" for a cancer treatment or a place in an elderly care home.

Had voters listened to Blair and his *eminence grise,* Mandelson. Who told them being outside The Euro would be the end of the world- or worse. Same as the *"Weapons of Mass Destruction"* they couldn't seem to find. And still The Elites got the illegal War they wanted, needed- just in time for an election. The whole *EU-topia* is a project of Fear. Rigidity, its cynicism that *They*- The Technocrats Know Best, will be its undoing. The EU has damned Europe to Balkanisation, then Islamification in the wake of its inevitable collapse.

If the EU Extremist had had their way, British taxpayers would now be paying to prop up the Dodo currency of the EURO. And its hidden cliff's edge of debt. As it is they subsidise corrupt regimes- Ethiopia's police state, the largest recipient of UK "aid" for example, via £13.6 billion of "Development Funds".

All paid for out of the *"Deductions"* at the bottom of *your* payslip. The British are The Mugs of the World. The Traffickers are laughing at your naivety as they speed past in a brand new Mercedes. Albanian drug-lords who built sumptuous their villas out of your wages, toast your generous idiocy. As one guide pointed out, asking me to guess how many yachts moored in a harbour Montenegro belonged to organised crime syndicates who made a "good living" out of EU kickbacks. She smiled. It was easier she said, to count the ones that were *not*.

"The Crisis" is not over – it has yet to begin. In fact, UK Taxpayers do fund The Euro- the Treasury siphons off taxpayers' money to support it via less obvious, increased contributions to the IMF and World Bank. Dishonesty, stealth is written into the very political DNA- the Constitution of the EU. The Constitution which remember, they rebranded as *"The Lisbon Treaty"*.

The Elites will do the same with Brexit. But "The Deal", like the EU itself will be a dangerously inverted pyramid of Hype. Short-term compromise after compromise, patched together with the usual media commentator's bull.

They can't understand why The People voted *"Wrong"*. They who earn £200,000 plus Expenses, in institutions such as The BBC, cannot understand the New World in which they find themselves. Marooned by their own smug, comfortable naivety and fixed ideas. But the Liberal Sun no longer orbits the Earth. Still they cannot "See or Hear no Evil" in their EU Bubble.

It is the Emperor's New Clothes syndrome. They do not, cannot, understand The Problem. Thing cannot return to a new normal, for the post-war Liberal consensus is over. It was living on time borrowed from others.

For their world is not the reality of queuing in the drizzle, for one job at ASDA- with 25 migrants behind and in front. Of waiting for a village bus that never comes.

Their Europe is social engineered. A parallel society of "Equal Opportunities". Except if you are  one of The Forgotten. A white British boy- the least likely to go on to higher education. Or a cushy career at the BBC. Who reports that scandal in the making?

Another world. Thinking they are being "Inclusive". Of 20% "BAME quotas". But "20%" isn't *Representative* of a village beside a B-Road to nowhere in Suffolk.  "Multiculturalism" drove on by. Past the Saxon church, built the last time there was an invasion by a spoilt Metro Elite. Their Quota is only "Representative" of a spoilt, arrogant few- of "People Like Us".

The Comfortable don't want their Party to end. But in the end, it is "Events" that as ever will burst the EU Bubble. The Dream. Or nightmare depending on which end of The Queue you are, for that job at ASDA...

The Elites inhabit another England. Of holidays at their second home in Cornwall with its weatherboard walls and stone floors painted in Heritage Green. The *Eliterati* are like The Rich- they are different from us. They can indulge their candy-floss insecurities in a £1.27m house on the "right side" of Barnes Common. Their children can always find a place at a "good" local- Private- school. And "Hubby's" job comes with BUPA health insurance if their wife gets sick. No need to resort to the reality of the The Queue again- at the NHS.

This is the real Divide. Not North and South. But a hidden *Inequality*. Unspoken. Not so easy to define. Of opportunity. The other England. The one not discussed *ad nauseam* over the polenta at dinner parties. They talk instead of of "Black Lesbian in Gender Transition", they know at work in the Sociology Department. Those less fortunate that they like the glow of "empathising" with over a glass of a "particularly rewarding" *Cahors. With its "Delightful flower tones"... They picked up a dozen bottles driving back last June... In case they slap on an export tariff, Darling...*

They pass the bus-stop in the Suffolk village which has never "Boomed or Bust". One of those scrappy "villages" you don't see in glossy features on "Dream Cottages". Like England itself, on the outskirts of a town, which is itself on the outskirts of somewhere else. Neither Built-up or Down. Country or *Urb*. Where a boy named Gary, they do not notice, waits for a bus into Ipswich that never comes. For an interview for a job he will never get. But at least as he has an EU Passport that confers him the Right of "Free Movement". The right to live in a deserted block-house, on the edge of a disused Soviet steel-mill in a Romanian town. "Two hundred miles from Anywhere"- as the locals say wryly- old men for there are no young men left- "And damn all when you get there"...

What a strange people the British are. In their Brave New England, Mr. And Ms Luvvie Believe. They fight for other people's Causes. For Everyone and Anything- except The Invisible English, ghost-like, all around them. Passing by, their head stuck inside their I-phone, talking to someone they do not know- a "Friend" in Kuala Lumpur they will never meet. Walking on the same street: but in an another country. What a waking nightmare we have made for ourselves.

"Mr. and Ms. Luvvie" of SW19 were on "The People's March" on Saturday. She teaches "Wellness" at £40 per hour. He is "between" breakdowns like all writers. Are they "The People", any more than their *Leave* voting neighbours? The ones they no longer want to speak to much. Or would lend their lawnmower as they did, the Summer before last. Before they discovered what their "Politics" were. What *sort* of people they were. And they *seemed* so nice. They even liked the dandelion tea. Or said they did. Until you got to know them. How could they vote Leave *and* have a rescue dog- Ms. Luvvie wondered?  Mr. Luvvie grunted something about taking an "instant dislike" to all Leavers- and Tories he met. "Because it saved time", he muttered.

It never occurs to Mr. Luvvie they might be helping create the very *Descrimi-nation* they so despise. Cultivating their *Ethnic* friends like rare orchids. Was so contrived. Collecting them like ornaments to display at suppers of the local Oxfam Group. They even wanted to get a "Refugee". Sudanese. Or better still- a Syrian. But as Mr. L pointed out he had his dust allergy and she they was "gluten-free"- so that might prove "Challenging" for the occupant of the box-room.

They flaunted their Right-On, tick-box, credentials. And glowed with self-satisfaction that at least they weren't like the "The Bigots" across the road. Even if they had to let their lawn become overgrown, pretending their lawnmower was "broken". The subterfuge, said Ms. Luvvie, would at least be good for the butterflies.

As if to prove how open-minded, Liberal Chic they are. Can afford to be in their open-plan kitchen- with its "real wood" floors of course, not laminate. Marching for The Minority whoever it is, just because they are a minority. For Everyone. Except if you no longer exist. If you happen to be a balding white man, in corduroy trousers a size too big. One of The Great Unwanted. An invisible, Ghost English. Surplus.

Those "Too Pale, Too Male", finding themselves Stateless. It is not *their* country now- but Anyone's and Everyone's. This alien-nation. English Refugees, exiled in their own country. Whatever their false passport says. They never wanted to be "EU Citizens". Just wanted. The Silenced who will not be silenced for another 50 years.

For now, The One Percent, The Smug, have the Power. The Voice. The Levers. Like the Wizard of Oz. Those who enjoy knowing how lucky they are. To live in a *nice* place like Guildford. Or leafy North Oxford, where *Remain* posters and *"Cup Cake Teas"* for Refugees, adorn every downstairs sash window. Those who live on the right side of the Park, dictating to those who cannot- How, What to think. While the EU illusion lasts. The *real* England is coming to a town near you.

# 6. Back in The EUSSR

The journey East by train was still like moving from Colour- into Black and White. Watchtowers may have been empty. Yet female train station managers still stood to attention, in full uniform and wartime medals, on windswept station platforms to salute- "The train from the West", as it passed by at 10.10 each and every morning. And border guards poked you in the ribs if you didn't produce your "Papers" fast enough.

Few realised then, as The Wall crumbled, that it would leave the last Soviet-style Political and Economic Bloc- The EU- intact on the Western side. The EU with its *"Growth & Stability Pacts"*. With all the paraphernalia of a Centralised, Soviet-era Federal Government desperately pretending it is not. Who will Liberate Europe, the EU28, from itself? The EU, by its very existence, has already caused the next European War. Micro-Wars in which your grandchildren will fight- whether they want to or not.

The irony is not lost on The Average Russian. It sometimes seems now, as if "The Wall" came down- on the wrong side. The EU remains, as the only truly "Communist" state in Europe. A state within a state, in the heart of Western Europe. Ironically, subsidised, and protected, by American taxpayers in Wisconsin, 4000 miles away.

Do not fall for the EU Illusion. The anti-democratic, corrupt and wasteful European Union's underlying motivation. It's crypto-Communist ideology, embedded in its foundation. Indelible. It is not possible to reform "Marxist-Leninism". Or The EU's hidden, symbiotic relationships with Organised Crime across Europe. It is erasing European Christian civilisation by stealth. As demonstrated in the EU's first proxy war with Russia in Serbia. By getting the public to remove it, memory by memory, Freedom by Freedom.


*"The EU will collapse not because of some profound Democratic principle: but because The US Declaration of Independence has some 1,300 words. Whereas, EU Regulations on "The Sale of Cabbages" contains 26,911 words".*

The EU regime keeps Europe infantilised. Unproductive. The few Washingtonian insiders who see the EU at all, view it, they tell me, as "28 Squabbling Teens". Slamming the door to their bedroom if they Can't Always Get What they Want... If they can decide what it is they *do* want. Instead of only what they don't. Expecting The US Bank of Mom and Dad, to pick up their dirty clothes. A taste of Isolation isn't always "A *Bad* Thing". As The Don might say.

What began as first as a *"Coal and Steel Trading Area"*, to move labour around Europe after 1945, has in two generations, as planned, become a new international State in all but name. Waiting for the "Brexit Crisis" of its own making, to reveal itself. The EU is controlled by, and for, a thin veneer of Elites in Business, Politics and the Media. Increasingly- one and the same. Whatever "Party" you vote for, you "Elect" effectively the same Government.

The minutiae of the privileged. The apolitical eunuchs, lounging in the harems of the EU Parliament in Strasbourg or Paris. Whatever The EU is or is not, History will remember it only as the end of the "Old Europe". A return to The Past, just when people were expecting The Future to arrive. People thousands of miles away are busy making other plans for their "Europe". The Westerners assumed that *Progress* would be something different. It turned out to be just the same exploitation, repackaged as "Consumerism". *"Choice"*. The Freedom to choose to be enslaved.

Whatever it proves to be, The EU and the Future, will not be the Democracy it never was.

# About The Author

*James Chanel is not "The father of two beautiful daughters, living Happily Ever After, in The Cotswolds- with an AGA"...*

His family arrived in India in 1799 to escape the guillotine. They remain- embroidered into the tapestry that is the subcontinent- by War, Fate and by marriage to the Nehru-Gandhi dynasty.

*He is the author of The Post-Raj Quartet- "The Beautiful People"- Why India has yet to gain its "Independence".*

**Biog. Papermedia 2017**



*A proportion of any profits is donated to GAW- Supporting Local & International Animal Welfare Charities and Projects.*

52